Just Between Us Girls

Poetry Celebrating Women

By

Wendy Grace Stevens

Just Between Us Girls: Poetry Celebrating Women
by Wendy G. Stevens.

ISBN 13: 978-1-945526-25-1
Library of Congress Control Number: 2018932647

Printed in the United States of America

I Street Press, 828 I Street, Sacramento, CA 95814

Wendy Grace Stevens also wrote
"The Poetry of an Ordinary Life" ©2016

This book is dedicated to my chosen sister, Carol Swan, and all my dear women friends, with a special wink to Winter's Children, those amazing gals on the A-Team; and to the two wonderful guys who have continually encouraged my writing. A special thank-you to Jim Hargrove for his PhotoShop expertise.

Table of Contents

Section I

Women, the Peacemakers

Love's Army

We are few, but we are mighty.
Motivated by love alone,
we will change the world.
Perhaps not all at once,
but slowly and steadily.
Our love will penetrate walls,
slip around barriers,
embracing each and every one.
We don't need to declare
a new war on anything,
or amass an army of marchers.
We don't need slogans or banners.
Love imparts meaning to
the most humble actions.
We will simply love,
wherever we find ourselves.
We will love because it is right.
Many things can change the world,
but love alone can change it for the better.

A Different Possibility

Political parties have their own visions,
Every religion its unique view.
So many ways to create divisions
And differentiate me from you.

There is a different possibility.
It's understanding, compassion, peace,
That echoes our inherent nobility
And allows all conflict to cease.

Let's each begin, right where we stand,
To embrace this worthwhile goal.
Let the love in your heart expand,
Sharing the peace that's in your soul.

Peace

In truth, there's a deep well of peace within us,
but sometimes it's hard to haul it up to the surface
when outer conditions seem hostile,
and tempt us to fight.
How, then, do we let the in-born peace of our soul
flood out into the world as an influence for good?
Even if we don't act in accordance
with our best intentions every time,
we need to acknowledge and encourage
even our weakest efforts,
because it does matter.
It's said the power of one person's loving vibrations
can offset the angry energy of a million others.
Whether or not it's true, that one among millions
will live a more peace-filled and happier life.

Language of the Heart

Language is dynamic, organic,
constantly changing to accommodate
new ideas, developments, and technology.
But the language of the heart
is eternal, constant, steady.
It speaks only words of love,
compassion, and kindness.
It knows no language barriers
or ethnic divisions,
recognizes no political differences
or national borders.
The language of the heart is heard
in the first sounds a baby makes
and in the last breath of the dying.
Let us each strive to speak only
the language of the heart
through all the days and years in between.

Section II

It's a Woman's Life

It's All About Me!

It really is all about me.
It's about how I look at life,
How I view myself,
How I relate to others.

My attitudes and beliefs
Color the pictures of my life,
And it's up to me to choose
Vibrant color or shades of gray.

It really is all about me!
How empowering to know
I can incline my world
Toward peace and beauty.

Princess to Potentate

What a perfect world it would be
If only everyone listened to me,
For I bear a message of love, you see.

When Princess Gwendolyn the Great
Is elected Whole World Potentate
The first thing I'd do is banish hate.

I'd ask every person to go within
And find love not just for kith and kin,
But for every one of their fellow men.

I'd bring about this new paradigm
And cause the Universe to realign,
Making life on Earth quite sublime.

Every child will be loved and well-fed.
Everyone will sleep in a nice warm bed.
Endless possibilities will fill their heads.

Compassion and kindness will rule the day
When Princess Gwendolyn has her say,
And the world will agree it's a better way.

Saturday Night

I feel discouraged and down tonight,
And I really don't know why.
Sometimes the blues come to visit me,
Most often when evening is nigh.

It's Saturday night, and I'm all alone.
Alone with my thoughts and my wine,
Wishing for a friend to visit and talk to,
Or better yet, a love to call mine.

Aloneness shouldn't be a dreadful curse.
I could put this quiet time to good use,
Like cleaning my desk or mopping the floor
Instead of using the blues for an excuse.

My life is actually quite fine, thank you,
With this one persistent exception.
I suppose whether one is lonely alone
Is simply a matter of one's perception.

Boxes of Life

My life is like boxes stacked on a shelf,
And each one holds a little bit of myself.
One box contains my workaday life.
Another holds past sorrows and strife
Keeping them safely hidden away,
Those experiences I don't want to replay.

My spiritual life is at the front of the stack,
And I open it daily to keep myself on track.
Time spent with friends has a great big box,
Holding laughter, tears and heartfelt talks.
Favorite activities have a place there, too,
Things I've already done, things still to do.

A special box holds my love for you.
It's tucked up high and out of view,
But brightly wrapped in unfailing hope.
The love within it helps me cope
With lonely days and lonely nights, too,
When I'd much rather be holding you.

Someday the door to my closet may burst,
And the boxes will tumble down headfirst
Disgorging a mass of tangled emotion.
Amidst all the chaos and commotion,
Perhaps I'll at last have the wisdom to see
The one I love most really should be me.

Self-Talk

If a friend spoke to me the way I speak to me,
I wouldn't be friends with her anymore!
I would never speak as unkindly to a friend,
Or even someone I might secretly abhor.

I must listen closely as I speak to me,
Imagine standing outside myself a while.
Can I find a more kind and loving way
To nurture my vulnerable inner child?

I should view her as my most tender part,
And ask what she wants and needs to hear,
And how she desires to express herself
To feel validated, loved, and secure.

I should always speak to myself with love,
Encouraging my child and my soul to grow.
If I don't show myself love and respect,
Why would others these things bestow?

Grace

For most of my life, I hated my name,
Even flatly denying it belonged to me,
Until one day its meaning dawned
And washed sweetly all through me.

The name I'd rejected reminds me now
Grace is the gift of Providence Divine.
Through Grace we live and love and thrive.
I'm proud to claim that name as mine.

Is it too late to say, "Thank you, Mom?"
To grow into Grace takes time and thought.
The light has begun to glimmer, and perhaps
Striving to live Grace fully won't be for naught.

River Rock

I want to be like a river rock,
one of those glistening cobbles
just below the surface of a pure,
crystalline mountain stream.
Rounded, gentle, with no sharp edges;
cleaned of the mud of resentment and anger;
free of the moss of the past.
Anchored securely in my life purpose,
yet finding pleasure swaying with the waves.
Solid, uncomplicated, authentic.
Like a river rock.

In the Garden

He knew she wanted to marry
and share life with a special love.
He liked his freedom to come and go,
and see her when it pleased him.

Still, she was lovely, with soft skin,
clear blue eyes and a beguiling smile,
bright with charm and intelligence.

"What a lovely place for a wedding,"
she mused, pausing in the beautiful garden.
"You make me feel pressured," he responded.
Looking up at him with a coy smile, she thought,
"Who said it had to be you?"

The Princess and the Pea

Like the princess and the pea, we pile pillow-top
mattresses onto the major problems in our lives and add
featherbed after featherbed over the lesser slights, slings,
and arrows, attempting to bury the hurt.

We hold ourselves together somehow through life's
huge challenges only to lose it over some seemingly
insignificant event. His cursing, her tears, are never really
about the Christmas lights that don't light, or the broken
heel of a favorite shoe.

We suppress our feelings when life presents us with real
difficulties--a frightening diagnosis, the loss of a loved
one, news of another mass shooting--perhaps because we
know that if the dam broke at those times, the reserves of
strength and faith required to see us through will be
depleted, leaving us adrift in a roiling sea, without
resources, without hope.

The small tragedies, though--the broken water pipe,
being alone at holidays--are safe enough outlets for
spilling pent-up emotions, feelings of loneliness and
inadequacy. One is freed to rage, to cry, to temporarily
succumb to the darkness without insurmountable
penalty.

Perhaps we should welcome these minor difficulties as necessary safety valves, allowing us to release enough emotion to preserve our sanity and equilibrium. It isn't necessary to light the exterior of the house for it to be warm and welcoming at Christmas time, just as eyes brimming with tears can still see the beauty of the holiday.

Butterfly

Finally, I'm the butterfly I was created to be,
proud to show my dazzling colors
and soar on hard-won wings.
Born into a cocoon of poverty and violence,
I struggled to escape,
not really knowing where escape lay,
or what was on the other side of its portal.
I envied others whose circumstances appeared
so much better, so much happier and easier.
I endured, not out of valor,
but because there was no other choice.
Little did I know that all butterflies must struggle
against the dark and suffocating confines
of their cocoon to awaken their wings,
to strengthen them and prepare for flight.
Do not mistake my joy for conceit.
It is the joy of humble gratitude
that all butterflies feel
as they float on the ecstasy of overcoming.

Lesson Learned

I didn't mean to cause offense;
I was actually quite concerned.
To make the situation even worse,
My sincere apology was spurned.

It's hard to watch a friend struggle
Without wanting to offer help,
But I guess it's best to remain silent
And let her resolve it for herself.

In the future I must remember
No one cares to hear my theory.
If she's really having a crisis,
She can call nine-one-one, or ask Siri.

Unwelcome Changes

What in the world is wrong with me?
I'm moody, lethargic, not who I used to be.
I miss my Self, my humor, my usual pep.
These days, my whole life feels out of step.

What caused this awful downward spiral?
For much too long I've remained in denial,
Trying to ignore this distressing trend.
Sometimes I feel I haven't even one friend.

I've no enthusiasm for life, it's just a struggle.
What used to cheer me seems too much trouble.
Here's the fearful question, stark and bold:
Have I slid into depression, or am I just getting old?

Amazing Young Women

The amazing young women of today give hope for the future. Self-directed, determined, strong, passionate and courageous, they carry forward the hopes and aspirations of their mothers.

Don't dare tell them they can't. They will show you they can. They can and they will bring merciful change to a world in need, a world too long enveloped in selfishness and warring energy.

They are warriors of a different sort, who believe in their dreams, dreams that are a beautiful testament to the power of love: dreams of equality, humanity, freedom, full stomachs and full lives.

They are ballerinas who climb mountains and fearlessly cling to cliffs, diligent scholars, firefighters, devoted spouses, musicians and ministers, and mothers who will pass on generations of hope, amplified by their own magnificence.

Beauty Within

Wouldn't it be nice if we all realized
The true beauty we possess
Has more to do with our inner selves
Than with our hair or dress?

It's healthy to want to look our best,
And show our most pleasing face.
But somewhere along the path of life
We must accept ourselves with grace.

Warts and wrinkles we've all got,
But those are unimportant parts,
Made invisible by the compassion
And kindness that fill our loving hearts.

Changing Times

When I was a little girl,
every young girl had a hope chest
where she kept the doilies
she'd crocheted and the tea towels
she'd embroidered to use
when she married,
and wore a diamond ring on her left hand.

Nowadays, single young women
buy themselves diamond rings
to wear on their right hands
indicating independence and success.

Divorced women of all ages
often have their diamonds reset
into bold new designs to reflect their changed status.

Today's intelligent women have hope chests, too,
where they keep their brokerage and bank statements
and a well-earned sense of self-worth.

Not Her Type

Quiet and studious, smoking a pipe,
The man was nice, just not her type.
How could she express that politely?
Or should she just say so, forthrightly?

He was persistent in his pursuit,
But her disinterest was resolute.
How could she say, while being kind,
No way would she change her mind?

Why do we fall for the ones we do
When we haven't even the slightest clue
That they're available or receptive?
Attraction isn't always perceptive.

What is the secret chemistry that selects
Specific members of the opposite sex?
And why is it not always by both felt
Causing hearts to simultaneously melt?

Through no particular reason or rhyme,
He fell for someone he thought sublime,
Only to have his high hopes falter.
She has no interest in a trip to the altar.

Section III

Girls Just Wanna Have Fun!

Yes, Sir? No Way!

Why do men assume they should tell
Women what to do, and how, as well?
If men only knew what women think,
Back to their caves they'd surely slink.

When a man expresses inflated ego,
Women know it's caused by his libido.
They know bluster is compensation
For some tiny part suffering disinflation.

Why do intelligent women tolerate this,
Resisting only when things go badly amiss?
Truth be told, as mothers we've got
Used to coping with a self-centered tot.

Shoes

Sometimes when I'm feeling sad,
Like I've kinda got the blues,
Somehow it makes me want
To go out and shop for shoes.

Macy's always has shoes on sale,
And it's a quick and easy drive.
Is it just my imagination,
Or was he waiting for me to arrive?

I know he saw the dark cloud lift
As I walked toward his display.
"May I show you what's new for Spring?"
I couldn't make myself walk away.

With my credit card safely stowed,
Smiling, I say "I'm just lookin'."
His eyes narrow, he's sizing me up,
Deciding how to set the hook in.

My shoe rack is overflowing,
I'm embarrassed to confess.
But those red sequined stilettos
Are something I must possess.

I drive home in elation,
New shoes beside me on the seat.
They're glamorous and gorgeous,
Even though they kill my feet.

I need a special place to wear them,
But gala nights out are only wishes.
Tonight I'll don them with my PJs,
And look fabulous doing the dishes.

My Evil Twin

I have an evil twin.
She has an evil way.
Does things I'd never do,
Says things I'd never say.

I've tried to disavow her,
To set myself apart.
I am kind and gentle.
She has a cold, black heart.

She'd cross a busy street
Just to kick a cat.
Behavior so despicable
I'd never stoop to that.

It seems that being nasty
Is the way she gets a kick.
I think she's completely nuts,
Twisted, gross, and sick.

Then while cowering in the corner,
My husband has the nerve to say,
"Honey, did you remember
To take your estrogen today?"

Cake Everlasting

Who says you can't eat your cake and have it, too?
Look at your hips, it's stuck there like glue!
What do you think makes your tummy bulge?
Could it possibly be you over-indulge?
Those chocolate eclairs, so moist and yummy,
Just coagulate and round out your tummy.
That half-bottle of Beaujolais Nouveau
Went right down last night with happy gusto.
The reason your pants no longer button
Is because you've been eating like a glutton.
So put down that glass of tonic and gin,
And head for the gym where you can begin
To work on those abs, your chins and thighs,
And get 'em back down to their former size.

Just Between Us Girls

This getting old is such a drag.
Today my boobs began to sag.
I don't know how they got that way.
They weren't like this yesterday.
Instead of uplifted, perky and round,
Suddenly they're pointing down.
Like a ski jump or a playground slide,
They're headed on a downward ride.
Daily showers were once delightful,
But now I find them almost frightful.
Obviously, to feel any cheer,
I must avoid nudity and the mirror.
I suppose if I got new boobs installed,
With my appearance I'd be enthralled.
But I'm sure it would hurt an awful lot,
So I'll just keep the ones I've got.
Yeah, I'm old, with wrinkled skin,
But the spirit of youth still lives within.
It's just not fair how my body acts---
My insides don't match the outer facts.

Pills

I don't need food, I'm stuffed with pills.
Five for arthritis and two for stomach ills.
Ibuprofen for pain in my creaky old knees.
More pills at night let me sleep with ease.

Mult-vitamins each day and calcium, too.
Fish oil and krill 'cause they're good for you.
Nothing about Metamucil makes me grin,
So I get it down mixed in tonic and gin.

To fight cholesterol, a daily glass of red wine.
My LDL's still too high, but I feel just fine.
One more tiny pill 'cause my thyroid is lazy.
Keeping track of them all is driving me crazy!

There really has to be an easier way.
Can't we just go back to an apple a day?
At my age, to complain I feel entitled.
Each encounter becomes an organ recital.

With a desire for health I've become obsessed,
To the point it's making me feel depressed.
But if with my doctor I discuss this affliction,
He'd probably give me one more prescription.

Celestial Starbuck's

When Starbuck's goes to Heaven,
All the beverages will be free.
No more paying four dollars
For your morning cup of coffee.

Whether your order's a simple cup
Of Java for Jesus straight,
Or a vente Latte for the Lord,
You'll never have long to wait.

Along with Americano Angelic,
They'll offer a Mocha for Mary.
And both will be available
With regular milk or non-dairy.

I'll go to Heaven someday,
And my dying wish will be
That Starbuck's got to Heaven
And set up shop before me.

Rubens Woman

Robust, athletic, a woman of substance,
Her name could be Athena, Juno, or Mercedes.
Tall and commanding, a well-rounded figure,
Not one of Weight Watchers' slender ladies.

In our culture where thinness is sought,
And sometimes taken to unhealthy extremes,
Others glance disapprovingly at the appearance
Of this oversized goddess in jeans.

Was she dropped into this era by mistake,
When the stork's large blanket unfurled?
Was she intended for a much earlier time?
She's a Rubens woman in a Twiggy world.

Cat Lady

Kitties on her windowsill
And in her reclining chair.
Her furniture is quite a mess,
Always covered in cat hair.

She rescues every stray she finds,
And says it's only for a day.
But kitties come and never leave,
'Cause she wants them all to stay.

All her neighbors know she's odd,
Without a lick of common sense.
She's just one cat short of crazy,
Say the gossips over the fence.

Christmas Cookies

Put the cookies in the freezer
Where they'll be out of sight.
As if that would solve my craving!
I hear them call to me at night:

"Oh, help, it's very cold in here!
But your tummy's nice and warm.
Come rescue us!" I hear them plead.
"One small cookie can't do much harm."

Sticking to a diet during holidays
Is very hard, but I keep on trying.
Though I'm sorely tempted to pretend
Rising numbers on the scale are lying.

Hair and Now

Grannies with white hair used to shine it up
Using Mrs. Stewart's laundry bluing rinse,
But instead of pristine white, the results
Were often startling blue or purple tints.

Ladies dyed their hair unnatural shades
Of maroon or blue-black to cover their gray.
Those unintended results are not unlike
What women purposely choose today.

Back then they curled their hair up tight
With stinky perms, a nearly all-day feat.
And now the style that's all the rage is
Straightening it with formaldehyde and heat.

It seems we're never satisfied with the hair
Nature designed and placed on our head.
We'll go to any length to make it look somehow
Different from what we got instead.

Kleptomaniac

She's a kleptomaniac, watch out for her,
Or you'll be missing something, too, for sure.
Watch your watch, your bracelet and rings.
She has a bad habit of filching things.

She took her roommate's goose-down vest,
Though it didn't even zip over her chest.
Roommate gave her one last chance,
Which she blew, and swiped her pants.

Section IV

A Woman's Place
White
Is In The ^ House

Closet of Good Intentions

I have a closet full of good intentions,
Half-done projects too numerous to mention.
Shoes and clothing that should be donated
Before they become hopelessly outdated.

A list of phone calls I really should dial,
Books I've meant to read for quite a while.
Bills and invoices, some paid, some owing,
And stacks of paper that just keep growing.

Every New Year I make the same resolution:
That this year I'll find a permanent solution
To the horror that awaits behind that door.
A resolution I resolutely ignore.

Brass Bed

For years and years I'd wanted
a bright and shiny brass bed.
Here was one right in front of me,
like the vision that danced in my head.
In the thrift shop window it stood,
with a price so amazingly low!
How could I possibly pass it by?
How I'd get it home, I didn't know.
That tiny price tag taunted me,
and lured me to make the purchase.
But that was only the start;
it quickly became a three-ring circus.
First I had to buy a bed frame,
and then, a new mattress luxurious.
By now I knew without a doubt
the price tag's lure was spurious.
I hired a painter to paint the wall
so that shiny brass bed would "pop."
Two-hundred-and-seventy bucks later,
it had a fitting backdrop.
Then the bedspread looked old and worn
and totally lacking class.
I didn't realize what I was getting into
when I bought that bed of bright brass.

One more shopping trip to the mall
would surely provide the cure,
to assure my big bargain brass bed
would shine in splendid allure.
I chose a bedspread, then, of course,
matching sheets were selected.
At last I was certain all the problems
with my decor had been corrected.
How wrong I was! For every item I bought
and proudly put on display,
Something else in the room looked tacky,
and in need of an upgrade.
My feet are sore, my credit card's smoking,
my wallet's completely deflated.
Oh, you beautiful, horrible brass bed!
What a monster you created!

Casserole from Hell

I invited friends for dinner;
they liked Mexican food.
So I prepared a casserole
from a recipe that sounded good.
I sliced and diced and stirred and
mixed and put it on to simmer,
while I made a salad and
poured the wine for dinner.

When I brought it to the table,
the aroma was delightful.
We gathered in anticipation
of that first tasty bite-full.
We gave our thanks and raised a toast,
as is our custom here,
to such a creative dinner host
and these friends gathered near.

We served our plates and took a taste,
and all decorum fled.
Tears filled my eyes, sweat wet my brow,
my face turned brilliant red.
Oh, my mouth, my tongue, my throat!
The burning wouldn't stop.
More than simply zesty and hot,
this fiery dish was over the top.

With nothing else prepared to serve,
and guests with hunger growing,
I raced to search the pantry,
my embarrassment was showing.
Desperate, I returned, and amid
muffled gasps and screams,
we ate eggplant-chili casserole
topped with maple nut ice cream.

The moral of this story,
if you think you really need one:
Never trust a recipe that says
"Serve on Halloween for fun."

Stormy Day

The electrical power is out
and a storm rages outside.
Sitting with a book by a bright window,
I yearn for hot cocoa
like my mother used to make
when we had thunder and lightning storms
back in Kansas long ago.
Unlike my sleek, modern kitchen,
we had an old gas stove then.
Hot cocoa is out of reach today.
I cannot go back, back to the cocoa
or to the cocoon of childhood.

Persistence

'Tho I try so hard to be efficient,
My efforts often seem deficient.
So many things on my to-do list,
And no one I can ask to assist.
I don't want to appear to whine,
But when I try to do chores on-line,
The spinning ball keeps going 'round
And my frustrations just compound.
Phone calls end in Please-Hold-Hell.
It makes me want to scream and yell!
Then I recall a well-worn platitude
That applies to my mental attitude:
"Whatever you resist, persists."
And I keep persisting to resist!

Temple of the Ants

My house obviously was built on a site sacred to ants.
Every time it rains, the descendants of long-forgotten
ancestors attempt to reclaim their ancient territory
and reestablish their sovereignty.
First come a few brave scouts,
seeking the surest and best route
for the full invasion force.
I do not allow them safe passage,
and when they fail to return to their units,
a full-fledged assault party comes hunting for them.
They march in confident formation
along the stove and across the countertops,
stopping now and then to investigate
any stray crumb or drop.
They inevitably appear when I expect company,
even though they're never on the guest list.
Ushering friends into a kitchen reeking
with the scent of Raid
isn't the warm welcome I prefer to offer.
A fortune awaits the genius who can transform
that distinctively unpleasant odor into, say,
the smell of apple pie, or cinnamon buns.
Or would that just attract ants?

Yard Work

I'm heading out to the backyard,
To wage war on those pesky weeds.
I'll yank them out by their very roots
Before they can set new seeds.

The vines overtaking my flowers
Will get a delicious but fatal treat.
I'll offer them yummy poison to drink
Before they discover my deceit.

I love a yard that's tidy and neat,
With shrubs and flowers galore,
And everything growing beautifully.
It's the work involved I deplore.

I'll kill the vines and rip out the weeds
And deadhead to complete satisfaction.
Or maybe instead I'll pour me some wine
And formulate a new plan of action.

Window

She sits at the window with her morning tea.
The lace curtain sways gently in the soft breeze.
Outside the window stands a magnificent oak,
century-old limbs swooning to the river beyond.
The river's placid pools reflect trees, blue sky, and
occasional clouds.

What does she contemplate?
The tree? The river? Her life?

Although she appears as soft and fragile
as the lace curtain,
like the tree, she has grown strong
through many trials and tribulations.
She stands firm in her strength and identity,
but like the river, she has learned to flow with life,
its currents, ripples and pools.

What is there to contemplate?
The tree. The river. Her life.

April Showers

It's April, and I'm motivated
To work out in the yard.
Squash and pansies will have to wait,
It's still raining very hard.

April's supposed to bring showers,
Not thunder and pounding rain.
After five years of dreadful drought,
I really should not complain.

But soon I'll want to travel,
When the weather's hot and dry.
The weather can change quickly,
And my lovely plants could die.

I've put in hours and lots of dough
To make my flowerbeds enthrall.
If this rain would just let up a while,
An irrigation system I'd install.

Section V

Outdoor Girls

Love Letter to the Sierra

Some say we came out of the sea,
Thus we're strongly attracted to its shore.
John Muir said, "Going to the mountains is going home."
That's where my heart wants to be, forevermore.

I praise the ocean for its life-giving role,
But at sea the view is endless and empty.
The mountains offer vast and varied views
That touch my soul ever so gently.

Winter's Children

Winter wraps its arms around us.
We are its children,
who see beauty in a clouded sky
and marvel at the majesty of trees
encased in glistening ice;
delight in the sight of snowflakes
falling from a sunny sky,
and revel in the abundant snow
in our mountain playground.

Old Broads Rule

We rule the slopes, the powder, the trees!
We rule with grins and whoops of glee.
We rule 'cause skiing gives us juice.
Like kids at play, we need no excuse!

We ski well and fast and fully engage,
Not modified by "for your age."
Ignore the white hair, don't be fooled;
On these mountains, Old Broads Rule!

Why She Skis

"Why do you ski?" he asked idly.
She closed her eyes to allow images
To fill her mind and form her words.
"The feeling of freedom," she said.
"It's like flying without wings.
The feel of the wind,
The sound of snow beneath my skis.
And the sights!
Oh, the views of mountain peaks
And trees frosted with snow.
The scent of pine when the day warms.
The feeling of being one with nature,
Intrepid, challenging myself."
She opened her eyes, dreamily;
He was gone.

Coyote

Skiing alone through quiet woods
That others choose not to enter,
Gives me time to reconnect
With the peace at my soul's center.

Seeking the best line of descent,
I pause now and then and find
My thoughts seem not to be my own,
But to come from a higher mind.

Beauty surrounds me everywhere
Here in the mountains and trees,
Where skiing feels like a dance,
Or prayer whispered on the breeze.

As if to reassure me that I belong
Here in this hallowed place,
A coyote appeared from nowhere
And looked right into my face.

It stared at me for a moment
Deciding if I'm friend or foe;
Then nonchalantly trotted away
Over silent, glistening snow.

Tree Skiing

Rising above the valley fog into a sunlit day
Of mystical beauty, crystalline and icy,
Like Christmas cards attempt to convey,
Welcomes one into the skiers' society.

Beyond reason, there must be an appeal,
A reward sane persons cannot discern,
That motivates skiers to pursue with zeal
Their passionate quest for the perfect turn.

Some skiers regard thickets of trees
Standing alongside the groomed run
As their natural skiing boundaries,
And others hear them beckon, "Come!"

Gliding silently through snow deep and light,
Through frosted evergreen and Aspen trees
That frame snow-clad distant heights,
Exhilaration and joy are found on skis.

Others may be puzzled by our quest,
But that gives us no concern or hesitation.
Winter exists to be enjoyed with zest
And skiers engage with eager determination.

Pink Sunglasses

He joined me in the chairlift, much to my distress.
I really didn't want him there, he was an awful mess.

His hair was red but graying; tangled, uncut and wild.
His outfit was mismatched and definitely not in style.

Tho' I tried to ignore him, he flashed a yellowed grin
Through the long, unkempt beard that adorned his chin.

He offered a "good morning" that I could not ignore.
Then I noticed the pink plastic sunglasses he wore.

I said, "Those glasses complete your outfit very well!"
He laughingly replied he thought they were pretty swell.

"I'd never buy them for myself, you can plainly see.
My seven-year-old daughter picked them out for me."

Suddenly my appraisal of this burly brute felt bad;
Instead of just a mess, I saw a proud and loving dad.

Paddling in the Sky

This morning I was transported
to a magical place.
My kayak floated through the sky
among puffy white clouds.
Sky-water as still as the
center of my soul
reflected the lake far below,
until a soft breeze ruffled
the calm water,
shattering my illusion
into a million sparkling ripples.

Walk on the Grass

Please walk on the grass.
It's even better in your bare feet.
Forget you've been carefully taught
To tread only on hard concrete.

Admire the dandelions growing,
The little mushrooms pushing through.
Enjoy this unkempt urban meadow
Nurtured by the sun and the dew.

No one comes to mow each week.
Native plants and flowers flourish.
It's a place where you can freely roam,
Allowing nature your soul to nourish.

Limerick

There was a young lady named Clare,
Who biked in the fresh morning air.
So far and so fast
She pedaled her ass,
She blistered her poor derriere.

www.ingramcontent.com/pod-product-compliance
Lightning Source LLC
Chambersburg PA
CBHW061509040426
42450CB00008B/1536